演式者：
李冠雄師傅是蔡李佛派功夫第五代傳人。
現任香港中文大學新亞國術會導師，
香港孔聖堂中學國術組導師，
香港國術總會永遠名譽會長兼裁判，
香港功夫協會副主席兼比賽顧問。

The performer:
Master Lee Koon-Hung
The fifth generation of Choy Lay Fut Kung Fu
Kung Fu instructor – New Asia Chinese Kung Fu Club, Chinese University of Hong Kong
Kung Fu instructor – Kung Fu group of Confucius Hall Middle School, Hong Kong
Honourable President and Referee – Hong Kong Chinese Martial Arts Association
Vice-Chairman and Competition Supervisor – Hong Kong Kung Fu Association

美術編輯：袁康就
Art Editor : Yuen Hong-Chau

The Spinning Spear of Choy Lay Fut Kung Fu

BY MASTER LEE KOON-HUNG

蔡李佛功夫

騰龍槍

李冠雄演式

騰龍槍

The Spinning Spear of Choy Lay Fut Kung Fu

0.	捧肘準備	Level elbow
1.	由膝批手	Swing arm downwards
2.	扎起抛掌	Ward off and skip, Throw Palm with Cat Stance
3.	執槍	Drag backwards
4.	仙人指路	Level the mouth
5.	扎起一扒一納	Block the left, skip and ward off with Cat Stance
6.	進馬槍	Advance, thrust forwards
7.	回頭攔	Sweep aside
8.	行	Ward off
9.	點水	Point downwards
10.	扎起納	Skip, ward off with Cat Stance
11.	進馬槍	Advance, thrust forwards
12.	跳起壓	Skip, ward off
13.	虎尾標	Punch forwards with the end
14.	扎起納	Skip, ward off with Cat Stance
15.	進馬槍	Advance, thrust forwards
16.	冚	Smash the right
17.	麒麟步單攔	Whirling Spear, slash to the left
18.	流水	Block upwards
19.	冚	Press the right
20.	槍	Thrust forwards
21.	跳起壓	Skip, ward off
22.	虎尾標	Punch forwards with the end
23.	扎起納	Skip, ward off with Cat Stance
24.	進馬槍	Advance, thrust forwards
25.	冚	Smash the right
26.	麒麟步單攔	Whirling Spear, slash to the left
27.	上馬流水	Advance, block upwards
28.	退馬吊馬扒	Retreat, block the left with Cat Stance

29.	截	Ward off
30.	進馬彈	Advance, press the left
31.	冚	Press the right
32.	圈冚	Circle press
33.	合馬槍	Close step, thrust forwards
34.	上右馬虎尾標	Advance, punch forwards with the end
35.	上右馬插秧	Advance, dig with the end
36.	點水	Point downwards
37.	扎起納	Skip, ward off with Cat Stance
38.	合馬一支香	Close step, thrust vertically upwards
39.	吊馬流水	Block upwards with Cat Stance
40.	冚	Press
41.	扭馬扒擺馬納	Twist Step, block the left, and Hook Stance, ward off
42.	上馬槍	Advance, thrust forwards
43.	獨脚截	Lift leg, ward off
44.	落馬彈	Advance, press the left
45.	換手兜	Parry upwards
46.	合馬槍花扎起一支香	Close step, Circle Spear and point upwards with Cat Stance
47.	擺馬壓	Twist Step, smash forwards
68.	扎起一扒一納	Block the right, skip and ward off
49.	上馬槍	Advance, thrust forwards
50.	回頭壓	Smash backwards
51.	扣馬陰槍	Advance with Hook Stance, Groin Spear backwards
52.	轉身兜	Turn, parry upwards
53.	扎起背槍	Shoulder the spear with skipping
54.	扣馬單攔	Hook Stance, Palm to the right
55.	吊馬閘橋	Chop Palm with Cat Stance
56.	掛搥收式	Hanging Punch and relax

0. 捧肘準備 Level elbow
1. 由膝批手 Swing arm downwards
2. 扎起拋掌 Ward off and skip, Throw Palm with Cat Stance
3. 孰槍 Drag backwards

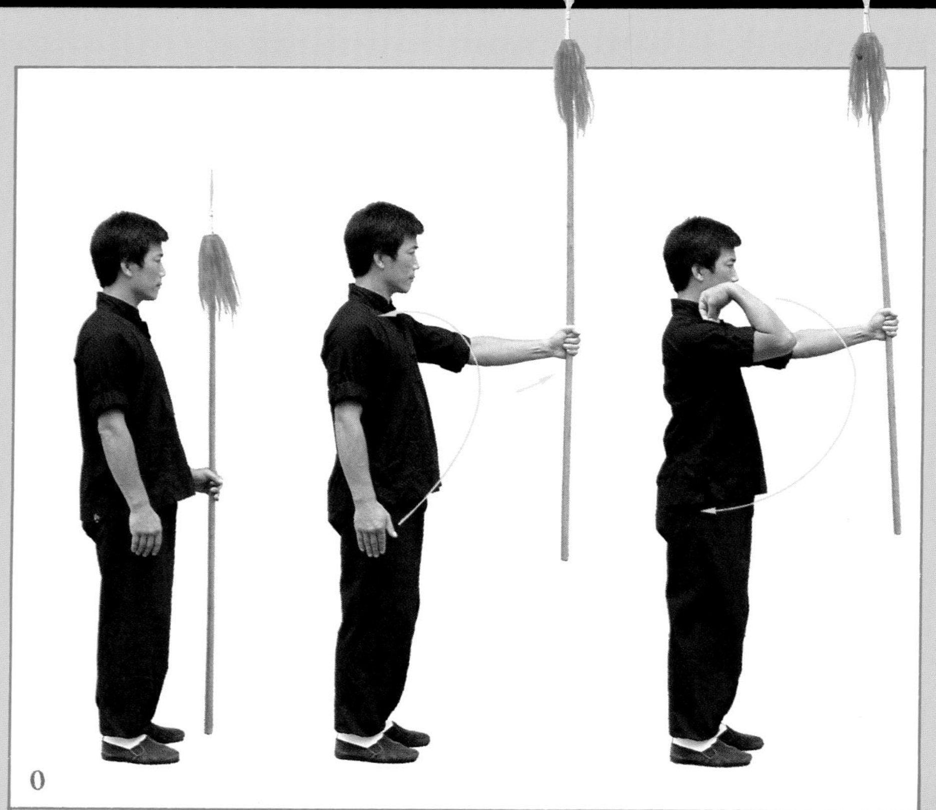
0

1

4

5

3

6

7. 回頭攔 Sweep aside
8. 行 Ward off
9. 黙水 Point downwards
10. 扎起納 Skip, ward off with Cat Stance
11. 進馬槍 Advance, thrust forwards
12. 跳起壓 Skip, ward off

7

10

9

11

12

13. 虎尾標 Punch forwards with the end
14. 扎起納 Skip, ward off with Cat Stance
15. 進馬槍 Advance, thrust forwards
16. 冚 Smash the right
17. 麒麟步單攔 Whirling Spear, slash to the left
18. 流水 Block upwards

13

14

17

15

16

18

19

20

21

25

26

APPLICATIONS OF THE SPINNING SPEAR

蔡李佛功夫 騰龍槍應用法

BY MASTER LEE KOON-HUNG
ART EDITOR: Yuen Hong-Chau
Demonstrators: Master Lee Koon-Hung and Master Yuen Hong-Chau

A **Refer to move 10 to 11, 14 to 15, 23 to 24,**
Ward off and thrust forwards:

1. Guarding position.
2. B advances and smashes forwards with his staff. A wards off at the left.
3. A circles down the staff and drags it to the right.
4. B is dragged violently off the balance.
5. A advances and thrusts forwards with his spear point.

演式10至11，14至15，23至24，一納一槍用法：

1.準備。 2.B上步剎棍。A圈槍。 3.A納槍帶回右邊。
4.B被拖走，失去平衡。 5.A進步扎槍。

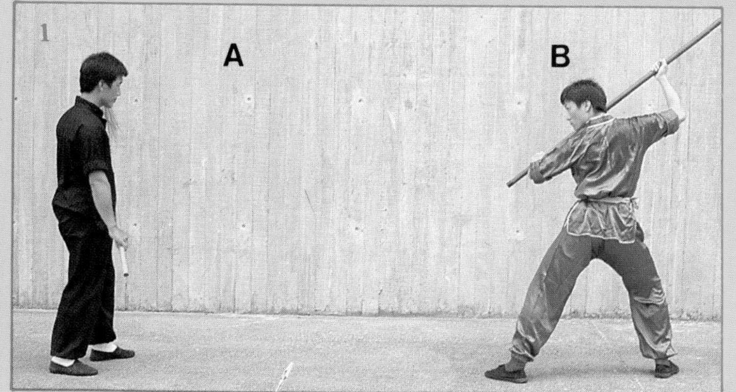

B

Refer to move 27, *Advance, block upwards:*

1. Guarding position.
2. B advances and smashes forwards with his staff.
   A wards off at the left.
3. B throws up the other end by borrowing the defensing force.
   A blocks at the right.
4. A immediately draws the spear point upwards towards the groin.

演式27，上馬流水用法：

1.準備。 2.B上步剁棍。A抽開。

3.B借力以棍尾橫剔。A轉右行。 4.A立即拋起槍頭，撩其下陰。

C

Refer to move 8 to 9, *Ward off and point downwards:*

1. Guarding position.
2. B advances and slashes forwards horizontally.
   A blocks at the left with his spear vertical.

3. 4. A turns his spear point downwards, scratching the face.

演式8至9，一行一點用法：

1.準備。

2.B上步橫掃棍。A左行。

3.4.A立即點以槍尖，刮在對方面部。

D

Refer to move 12 to 13, 21 to 22,
Ward off and punch forwards with the end:

1. A thrusts forwards with his spear point. B wards off forcibly.
2. A draws up the spear end by borrowing the pressing force.
3. The spear end blocks against the staff.
4. A steps forwards and punches forwards with the spear end.

演式12至13,21至22，跳起壓、虎尾標用法：

1. A持槍刺出。2. B彈棍擋之。3. A借力翻起槍尾。
4. A上步以槍尾撞向B的頭部。

E

Refer to mive 19 to 20, 32 to 33, *Press and thrust forwards:*

1. Guarding positon.
2. B thrusts forwards with his staff.
3. A circles the spear and presses heavily against the staff.
4. B leaks an open space, and A quickly thrusts forwards with his spear.

演式19至20，32至33，[illegible]、槍用法：

1. 準備。
2. B進棍。
3. A圈[illegible]。
4. A順勢彈入。

F

Refer to move 18 to 20,
Block, press and thrust forwards:

1. B thrusts forwards with his spear point.
   A circles down the opponent's spear.
2. B's spear is sprung off.
3. A quickly thrusts forwards with his spear.
4. A's spear stabs at the throat.

The alternatives:

4. Borrowing A's force, B circles up his own spear.
5. B immediately thrusts forwards with his own spear.
   A presses B's violently.

6\. 7. B's spear is sprung off without control.
A thrusts forwards with his spear point towards the throat.

演式18至20，流水、冚、槍用法：

1. B進槍。A攔槍迎擊。
2. B槍被帶開。
3. A立即扎槍。
4. 槍刺中喉部。

或有如下用法：

4. B借力圈起。
5. B隨即扎槍。A拿槍重重冚下。

6.7. B槍失去控制。A扎槍刺向喉部。

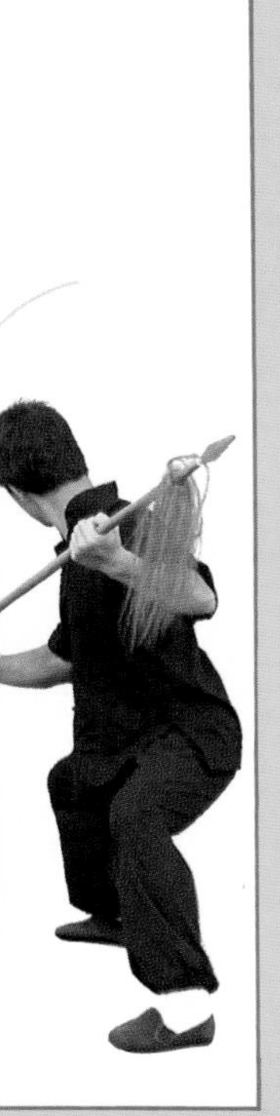

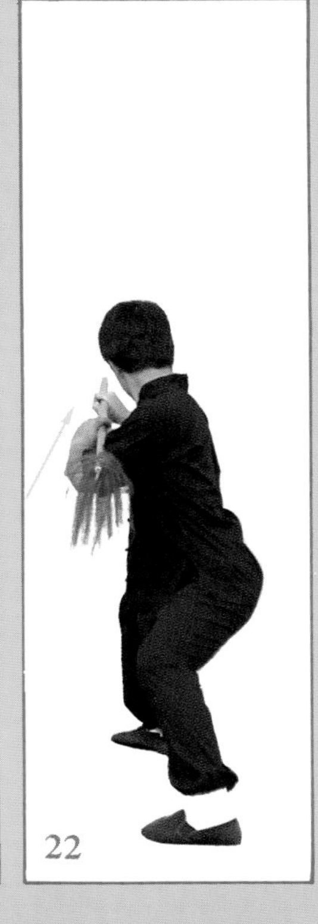

22

23

24

27

28

32

33

30

31

34

35

36

37

38

41

42

39

40

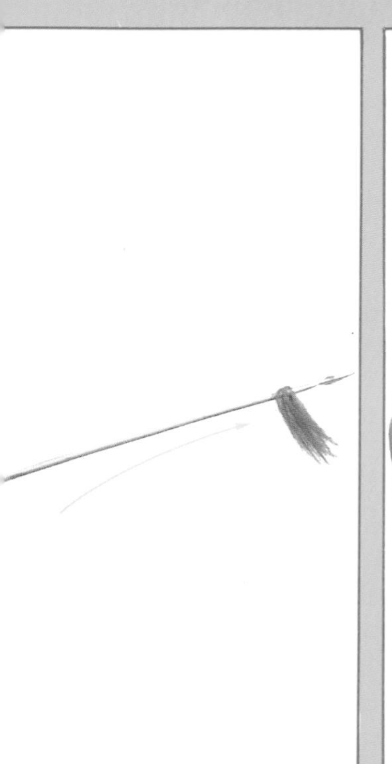

43

44

45

46

47

48

51

49

50

53. 扎起背槍 Shoulder the spear with skipping
54. 扣馬單攔 Hook Stance, Palm to the right
55. 吊馬閘橋 Chop Palm with Cat Stance
56. 掛搥收式 Hanging Punch and relax

53

54

55

文武合一

二千五百多年前，孔子提倡君子志於道，據於德，依於仁，游於藝，從而尋求人生完美的境界。當時君子務須具備六藝之修鍊。此六藝爲禮、樂、射、御、書、數。其中射御二藝乃追求身體及心智的發展。

今日，六藝被視爲發展完人理想的條件，爭取德、智、體、羣的均衡。從前，文武全才者往往被認爲是效忠國家之適當人選。同樣，今日的社會亦需要此等通文曉武的人才，投入有意義及積極的服務，比方外交、軍事等。我們秉承儒家主張文武兼備的精神，繼往開來，努力不懈鍛鍊中國功夫，並以嚴謹的態度鑽研學問，以求達到這崇高的理想。

More than 2,500 years ago, Confucius advocated that all gentlemen should seek the ideal of personal perfection, aspiring to the Way, abiding by virtue, adhering to benevolence, and pursuing the arts during leisure. In ancient times, gentlemen were required to perfect themselves in six arts : rites, music, archery, charioteering, calligraphy and mathematics. Two of the six, namely archery and charioteering, were pursuits for the development of physical as well as mental fitness.

In modern times, pursuit of the six arts has come to mean the development of a well-rounded person who strives to achieve an orderly balance in his intellectual, physical, social and moral aspects. Just as in ancient times, gentlemen who excelled in learning and physical arts were judged the most able to serve the state, today those who have mastered learning and the martial arts are capable of contributing to society in a meaningful and positive manner, whether they choose to serve in diplomatic, military or other capacities.

In the same spirit that Confucius wisely urged the men of his day to acquire a balance of mental and physical perfection, we today continue to strive for that perfect balance by the disciplined practices of Chinese Kung Fu and the disciplined mind and attitude towards learning which make all things possible ....